The Epiphanies

VOLUME 1

EDWARD UCHIMA UCHE

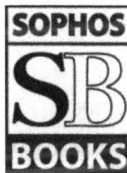

SOPHOS
SB
BOOKS

The Epiphanies (Vol. 1)
Copyright © 2024 by Edward Uchima Uche

Published by
Sophos Books
Croydon
sophosbooks.com

ISBN 978-1-905669-44-8

Cover design by *Tope Enoch*
Printed in the United Kingdom

CONTENTS

*To the woman who ignited
the flame of creativity within me,
my dearest mother, Charity Uchegbu.*

ACKNOWLEDGEMENTS

Being my first book, my appreciations are many, each one from the heart. My highest thanks goes to God Almighty who enriched me with the knowledge that birthed this book.

I am grateful to my father, Friday Onyedimma Uchegbu, whose countless sacrifices have been the bedrock of my journey to becoming who I am today. My mother, Charity Uchegbu, opened the doors to a world of words and wonder that transcended the limitations of any classroom. You filled our home with the magic of poetry, making every day a lesson in the beauty of language. Thank you, Mom, for being not just a teacher but a source of endless encouragement and support.

Thanks to my incredible wife, Lovelyn Imabong Edward, whose support and encouragement fuelled the journey of compiling my nuggets and stories into a book.

Thanks to Pastor Mrs. Juliene Afolabi, whose wisdom and steadfast support were instrumental in transforming the raw manuscript into something meaningful. Your belief in me is a constant source of inspiration.

To Eucharia Lucy Okpara, a friend and meticulous proofreader extraordinaire, your keen eye and dedication added much value to this work.

To my enduring friend, Engr. Danisa Olulade, you continue to push me beyond my perceived boundaries.

I am grateful to Engr. Charles Abangwu and my erudite friend, Evangelist Amara Okore Owotemu. Your constructive critiques and feedback guided me through this creative process.

Thanks to my muse and confidante, Kaylah Uche. You inspired me with stories of how *my* pursuit of excellence has strengthened and energised your own endeavours.

A heartfelt thank you goes to Pastor Tokunbo Emmanuel, who not only saw the potential in my work, but also provided the platform for it to reach a wider audience. Your expertise and commitment to the craft have been invaluable.

1

SINCERITY

*My principle is to avoid what I cannot concede;
my wealth is the value I place on sincerity.*

There is no miracle to being sincere than thinking through the pros and cons of plans before we put them into action. The major challenge for many of us is that we often fail to think through the consequences of our actions before taking them.

Sometimes, you need to gauge yourself against every lie you have told, every dubious engagement, and all the secret actions you cannot confidently admit if they were brought to light. When you do this from a place of honesty, you will easily realise that those actions do not truly reflect who you portray yourself to be, and this is exactly why you cannot wholeheartedly take responsibility for them.

I don't think there is any humiliation that can be as severe as self-humiliation stemming from getting caught while engaging in some actions you cannot bring yourself to accept. Nothing impoverishes maturity more than insincerity. Life's experiences and the unfolding mysteries of existence have taught me the value of rational thinking, a lesson that prevented me from getting to a point where I would have to perverse truth to salvage my reputation. This forms the bedrock of my ideology about maturity.

To evaluate your thoughts with objectivity, it is crucial to introspect and distance yourself from them. Judge your thoughts without bias based on the action point, the positive and negative outcomes, people's reactions, and your willingness to take responsibility, irrespective of how others perceive it. By the time you are through with this unbiased reflection, you will be better equipped to determine whether a proposed action is worth pursuing or not. Be known for sincerity because it is always beneficial no matter the circumstances.

My guiding principle is to refrain from accepting or endorsing things that do not agree with my beliefs and convictions. To me, sincerity is my true wealth. It is a value I hold in high esteem. In other words, I believe that honesty and authenticity in my actions and interactions with others are more important than amassing material wealth or success at the cost of compromising my beliefs.

2

CRITICISM

Even the dead are criticised; the only difference is that they don't say a word.

If you think you are the only one facing denigration, it is time to reconsider. Someone once told me that, "If you see anyone being highly criticised and denigrated by a good number of people, he or she is outstanding; it could be outstandingly good, or outstandingly bad." In life, regardless of which category you fall into, people will definitely talk about you.

It is essential to recognise that criticism is a major weapon often deployed by rivals to slow you down to their level or even below. So, regardless of the view of your critic to denigrate or correct you, use it as a drive for growth. Criticism can help you right your wrongs and can also make you stronger. However, never allow it to bring you down, because being vilified for ascending to higher heights is better than being denigrated for condescending to mediocrity.

You must understand that no man, not even the dead, is immune to criticism. People will often criticise others and pass judgement on them, even if they are no longer alive to defend themselves. The only difference is that the dead cannot respond to the criticism directed at them. In essence, criticism is an integral part of life, and it is something that everyone, whether dead or living, will face.

3

MORALITY

The approval of absurdity by 99.9% of the world's population can never moralise it.

A Nigerian adage holds that, "If a particular wickedness prevails for a while, it develops into a tradition."

It deeply disturbs me whenever I see a supposed custodian of morality and godliness succumb to depravity due to the prevailing views of their society. No matter how one may try to justify it, the components or values of morality are not dynamic. They are not subject to societal definitions. Instead, they are grounded in fundamental qualities such as compassion, hard work, self-respect, respect for others, gratitude, kindness, charity, honesty, cooperation, responsibility, and generosity.

I advocate for being guided by the moral values inherent in its definition and implementation, rather than bowing to societal pressures that may lead to a mix-up or redefinition of its constituents.

Today, many respected societies have incorporated certain aspects into their constitutions. However, it is essential to question whether such inclusions qualify them as moral.

Any trend that defies the values of morality is definitely an undesirable social influence, irrespective of the number of people who approve of it. Morality remains a steadfast phenomenon that does not change based on popularity or the passage of time. And the fact that the majority may vote against it does not diminish its value or change its status.

So, a worthwhile and acceptable standard should not be determined by the number of those who accept it. Instead, it should be evaluated based on the scale of compassion, hard work, respect (both for self and others), gratitude, kindness, charity, honesty, cooperation, responsibility, and generosity.

4

WORDS ARE POWERFUL

"Nothing imprisons proficiency like high walls of despondency, and unending denigration; she is short-lived without the breath of motivation and dies without the smell of success."

I t is absolutely difficult for a dream to strive in the presence of discouragement, mockery and constant failure, no matter how worthwhile it is. The absence of results and encouragement for genuine efforts can reduce commitment over time, potentially eliminating the likelihood of long-term success.

Sometimes, we underestimate the value and impact of words like, "Well done", "You're doing great", "you can do it", etc. It is absolutely challenging for a dream to flourish in an environment of discouragement, mockery, and constant failure, regardless of its value and worthiness.

Words are so powerful that they can drain and dissipate one's energy and eventually constitute a showstopper to an objective or goal. At the same time, it is so powerful that it fuels our cold passion for objectivity.

5

IMAGINATION IS NOT ENOUGH

*Motivation, courage, and willpower are the
undeniable forces that propel a venture from when
its success is only an imagination.*

I f success in all our life pursuits were just a
function of our thoughts and imaginations, I
doubt if any ordinary person would fail in
their endeavours. Many of us have constructed
and completed magnificent skyscrapers and
built great business empires generating
millions of income, all within the realms of our
heads. However, the reality of every dream
requires more than thoughts or imagination; it
demands motivation, courage, and self-
determination to start somewhere, even when
the starting point appears to be nowhere.

Every rewarding venture is preceded by a vision that comprises a starting point and an outcome called success, but the heartbreaking truth is that while some of us have these great pictures and projects in our minds, we may never advance further beyond mere imagination. Some may express these imaginations verbally but never take a concrete step to bring them to life. And for some of us, we seek motivation, employ courage, and exercise willpower to deploy these images from our imaginary world to reality.

There exists an empty space between every vision and its success that requires commitment to bridge the gap between the two. What sets commitment in motion, closing the gap, is motivation, courage and willpower.

6

AN ALLY IN EVERY PHASE

In every course and undertaking of life, there is always an ally heading your way, no matter the hour of the day you step out.

In any endeavour you wish to embark on, you will encounter people that will encourage you. If you want to be productive, there are people who are readily available to help you. Likewise, if you want to be unproductive, there are people who are waiting to assist you in that direction. Even when you undertake novel pursuits, you will find someone to encourage you all the way. However, the ultimate task of accomplishing your goals lies with you.

The wife of a friend of mine got a

scholarship to do her Master's degree in Biomedicine (Biomedical Science) in Brussels, Belgium. At the point of rounding off, she applied to do her PhD in the same school in the same course, but her application was not honoured on the grounds that they had limited admission for the course, which were specifically for students from French colonies. Faced with this setback, she almost settled for an alternative option. However, on second thought, she wrote to all the nearby European universities that offered the same course. Fortunately, a German university offered her admission to the course.

By the time she graduated from the Belgian school, she turned out to be the best graduating student of that set. The school then appealed to her to stay back for her PhD, but she turned down the offer because someone (a German woman) had gone out of her way to get her temporary accommodation pending when she would be able to rent a place.

There is always someone out there willing to offer assistance and support when you step out. However, what you are stepping out for determines your ally as well as how, where and when you can reach them. If your pursuit is worthwhile, you will spend some quality time to earn your ally's attention because talk is cheap, and nobody will take you seriously until you prove your seriousness and ability.

Therefore, in whatever you want to do, if you can lay the bricks of greatness in your mind, helpers are available to help you lay them up in reality whenever you are ready.

7

MASKED WOMEN

*"The heart of a woman is like a deep sea.
You only see what comes to the surface,
unless she takes you deep."*

Sometime in the past, a beautiful young lady approached me for a favour and I obliged her. We became intimate along the way, and from there, we became business partners and would later share a three-bedroom apartment. Although we spent most of our time together as intimate friends, business partners, and apartment mates, I only knew a little about her background. But then, I still believed that there was reciprocal trust between us.

Four years down the line, based on the assumption of mutual trust, understanding, and love between us and a strong sympathy for her untraceable family identity, I decided to get married to her. But I demanded to learn about her family, including how and where she grew up. To my surprise, she told me to forget about her background. She insisted that I should pay her dowry (bride price) to the church she attended then, but I told her it was impossible.

As Africans, or Nigerians to be precise, we don't marry on the street. I told her we get married into a home. Besides, no human emerges from the woods. I told her, "At every point in time, someone must have known you. You went to school with other people, you fed and existed in a home, you bought things from the market, and you walked on the street. So there must be something to tell me about your past to justify taking your dowry to a church. Also, there must be something to tell my parents to justify matrimony with you."

After dilly-dallying for two weeks, I was already running out of patience and understanding with her at this point, she came up with a story that hoodwinked me into brokenness. I agreed to pay her dowry to the church. What I didn't know was that the real story was hidden behind a beautiful mask.

A few days before the marriage meeting with the church, a military officer came into the scene and made us split. Apparently, she was seeing him while we were together. Some years later, I got a call from a young man in Abuja who introduced himself as that military man. Among the many discussions we had, he apologetically told me things I didn't know about her all through the four years of our relationship.

The experience taught me that women are highly secretive when they want to be.

8

TIME COUNTS

"The minus of yesterday is usually the shortage of today and may result in the emptiness of tomorrow if not recovered today."

The minus of yesterday means different things to different individuals. It could be the apologies we failed to offer those we offended, which then snowballed into a bigger challenge we struggled to handle. It could also be the mismanagement of time, values, and opportunities that has left you stranded today. Many people are so caught up in the web of yearning for the things they have been deprived of for a long time that they forget the privileges bestowed upon them by age and time. Consequently, they fail to remedy the situation until nature invades their lives and worsens their situation.

Certain things work like a time bomb and every second counts. Also, the best opportunity to survive is at the moment you hear the first beep. You either disable it or escape at once.

Life is like a relay race. If the baton is not properly handed over to the next anchor and it falls to the ground, his ability to pick it up as quickly as possible, in accordance with the rules of the game, determines whether his team will remain in the race. It also affords him the chance to win because every minute counts. Any act of insensitivity to time and its cost implications will result in the loss of time and, subsequently, the loss of the trophy.

Parents and guardians owe their children and wards some vital responsibilities that prepare them for the subsequent phases of life. However, it's important to recognise that fulfilling these responsibilities isn't always guaranteed. As a result, one should not feel disheartened or defeated if these gaps are not filled, leading to undesirable vacuums.

Some individuals tend to blame their parents for their inability to acquire an education. Some blame their parents for their financial struggles, citing a lack of inheritance as an obstacle. I have also seen people who did not inherit a wooden spoon, yet they work hard to create better opportunities for themselves and their families.

I know someone who struggled against all odds to go to school. He had to share truck space with cows during visits from the Northern part of Nigeria, where he was doing his youth service, to Western Nigeria, where his widowed mother and siblings lived. He would alight from the truck, smelling like cow dung and urine. He even felt too embarrassed to board a local bus (Moluwe) after being dropped off at the cattle market, miles away from his home in a Lagos suburb. Nevertheless, he persisted and fought against all odds to achieve his goals.

He persevered throughout those years of his academics and youth service to ensure that the absence left by his father's untimely exit did not diminish his and his entire family's chances of a fair living. Today, he can travel first class to any part of the world he desires.

Another individual with an amazing testimony is Nick Vujicic, an Australian born with tetra-amelia syndrome (a rare disorder characterised by the absence of all four limbs). He is one of those people born without the slightest ray of hope for survival, but he held on to the power of creation, residing within him, to invent hope in a hopeless situation and the courage to take a step of faith without limbs. Today, he is one of the most celebrated televangelists in the world. In a realm of total visible emptiness and a defenceless frame of mind, he forged a path to absolute independence and abundance for himself and those around him.

So many people who are born a hundred percent more able than Nick Vujicic have chosen to magnify their disabilities and the impact of their family challenges in their lives, consequently leading to a profound emptiness that may never be filled in their lifetime.

9

SERVANT TODAY, MASTER TOMORROW

I do not ask to be treated as a prince within me, but while I await my appearance, honour me and my service, just as an honourable servant serving a fair master.

I belong to the school of thought that believes that the final destination of a man is not the function of his present location but a determinant of his inexplicit crude destiny, the vision of his mind and his effort to reach it.

There is no end without a beginning, and there is no great end without a little beginning. Every great achievement you see today once existed only in the mind of the achiever, who was probably regarded as a nonentity. My understanding of intelligence is the ability to appreciate and show regard to every human being, as long as he or she still breathes.

I recall going through the excerpt of the biography of Dr Cosmos Maduka, the chairman of *CosCharis Group*. He used to tell children who mocked him each time they passed in front of his uncle's workshop, where he was an apprentice at the age of nine, that he would be better than them in six years. It was as if he planted a tree of success that would mature and bear fruit in six years. Between the fifth and seventh years of his apprenticeship, just as he had optimistically confessed, his uncle, without perceiving the inexplicit princely personality in him, amusingly gave him N200 to establish his own business, merely because he attended a church programme, even at that age.

Unbelievable for a child his age, but he looked at his uncle in the face and said to him, "God hardened the heart of Pharaoh to show his might in the land of Egypt. I served you well, and I don't deserve this, but if this is what you have to offer me five years from today, you will be amazed." And the rest is what we see and know about the *Coscharis* group today. He held onto his vision and strategised his mission, undeterred by his mates' mocking remarks about him being a little mechanic boy. Luck played a role, and his uncle perceived him as a thorn in the flesh instead of a prince in the making. He impoverished him and undermined his skills and servitude.

One day, while discussing the uncertainties of life with my friends, one of them shared a story about his former colleague at one of the biggest oil companies in Nigeria. He resigned his appointment as a junior staff because the company employed a little girl as a senior staff member. This little girl had grown up before him in his boys' quarter, living with her elder brother, who acted as her guardian. He obviously didn't see that coming because, back in those days, she would greet him in his compound whenever she walked past or after returning from school, often wearing a thorn skirt and a worn-out shirt. If only he had known what the future held for her, he might have been nicer during those encounters.

Beware of how you treat people, because your servant today may be your master tomorrow.

10

A NATURAL MAN

A challenge does not necessarily cause a "naturally" good man to turn evil; but it rather awakens the residing evil in a naturally good man.

There is an inherent evil residing in every natural man, which is awakened by adverse challenge and pressure. The goodness of a man without Christ is akin to any other prevalent human factor in his world, often induced by the circumstances he finds himself in. Belief (faith) is a formidable force that moulds the ideology of people and, as such, influences their reactions on different occasions. Being a good man transcends beyond natural reactions to appreciable things. It is reflected in what you do when you are pushed to the wall.

A friend of mine once said, "You cannot say that criminality is not in you, until you are exposed without limitation, to an attractive and well-designed opportunity." Everybody can do what is good, but not everyone is good all the time. The capacity to remain good constantly depends on what governs your inner self, not the influence of your surroundings or prevalent circumstances around you.

Remember, that something being deemed acceptable by human law or society does not inherently signify its goodness. In other words, the ability to do what is right and good, irrespective of circumstance, is dependent on how much of Christ is inside of you.

A natural man is ruled by natural circumstances, which expose him to emotional and attitudinal swing.

11

FAME

A man's unquenchable thirst for fame and unrestrained lust for affluence keeps him from waking up to morality.

It is a mark of wisdom to know where and when to draw the line in everything we do. A Nigerian adage says, "A stubborn fly ends up in a grave with a corpse." There are two forces that determine the fame of a man: the force of good and evil. The principle of the force of good encourages reference and value for morality and humanity as a means to fame, while the spirit of evil has no regard for morality and humanity but rather esteems fame above all things.

I once read about a young man who

deliberately committed a heinous crime and surrendered himself to the police, solely to achieve fame by appearing in news headlines. Another young man engaged in a serious financial fraud to fulfil his childhood vow to his friends. He had always pointed to a specific spot whenever they walked back from school, promising to construct an edifice there that would serve as a landmark in the entire community, and thus, make him renowned.

My friend Adah Akenji, a Cameroonian Singer, producer, and songwriter, who once lived with me, expressed his desire to be famous. However, he emphasised that he would not pursue fame at the present cost of compromising his moral values and relationship with God. Adah received numerous offers, but he remained steadfast in his decision to prioritise his principles and faith over temporary popularity.

Hypothetically, fame is like a diamond securely held within a beautiful, transparent vault. This vault is protected by a set of codes known as moral and integrity, which can only be obtained from a custodian known as the spirit of good with a currency called conscience. However, lurking in the shadows is the spirit of evil, armed with a sledgehammer, seeking to influence and tempt individuals into destroying the vault's lock and looting the diamond. The purpose of this sinister act is to discredit the spirit of good and undermine those who truly deserve the diamond. It requires a person with an unquenchable thirst and unrestrained craving for fame to succumb to the spirit of evil, abandoning moral principles and integrity, and to loot the diamond.

If you chase fame without caution, you will probably cross the boundaries of morality, either consciously or unconsciously. When people say they must succeed by all means, they disregard moral considerations. And at that juncture, they can do anything to succeed.

12

HEART CONTENT

Each time I stand before the world, I stand naked. Some people choose to see my nakedness through macroscopic glasses, some through microscopic glasses, while the noble at heart choose not to see me beyond my outward apparel. However, the only thing that is truly veiled in me is my heart.

Everybody is aware of gender differences, and the mental image of these differences often fuels the foolishness of sexual lust. Though one can easily discern another person's gender at first glance, true individuality remains concealed until one unveils their true self. The essence of who we are lies not in our gender but in the contents of our hearts. Gender cannot explain a person's character traits or godliness. Good and evil deeds are not restricted to a gender; both can be exhibited by anyone. Intimate encounters may occur between a young man and a young woman, yet genuine understanding of each other remains absent.

A lot of people have faced misunderstandings due to dealing with people who knew their genders, backgrounds and other obvious information about them, but never bothered to know the content of their hearts. Similarly, many others have lost worthwhile friendships and relationships because they were more concerned with their preconceived views of these individuals and never bothered to know the essential aspects about them until they let them slip away.

People have lost their lives because they saw beautiful damsels and handsome young men outwardly, thinking they knew them solely based on their gender and attractive appearance. However, when these individuals unveil their true personalities, they destroy their victims via poison, infidelity, charm and witchcraft. Some have unknowingly embraced seemingly humans who met their demise because they never knew they welcomed snakes.

Outward appearances can be deceitful, but the genuine personality of every individual lies inward. To discern the true nature of a person and to recognise your real friends, an understanding of God is essential.

13

LIFE IS FULL OF SUSPENSE

Suspense is part and the beauty of life; you either wake early, get dressed in expectation of its tension, or die early overriding its mystery and uncertainty by inventing and living in the artificial, forsaking real life.

Life on earth is a mystery that is tied to time, and it deserves total commitment and endurance to unfold because God can never write or produce a tragic story. There might be different points of suspense and climaxes for different plotlines, but He is perfect in ending every story well, including yours.

> "For I know the plans I have for you," declares the Lord, "plans to prosper you and not to harm you, plans to give you hope and a future."
>
> **Jeremiah 29:11**

At a time in Lagos, the easiest and quickest way to journey within the metropolis was to travel through the state government-designed special route via a special commercial transport known as BRT bus. Thanks to this route, you could avoid traffic congestion and slowdowns. Consequently, you would always encounter a queue at their terminals throughout their operating hours. They did not have a specific time of arrival, but your chance of boarding the next available one depended on your position in the queue relative to the bus's capacity.

Some people would spend one hour, waiting for their turn in the queue, and when they succeed, they reach their destination in the next thirty minutes. Ironically, others who lack patience decide to jump into any other available bus, loudly declaring their locations. These people often end up spending three hours or more stuck in traffic congestion. They would refuse to join the BRT bus, even if it could take them closer to their destination, as they are determined to either reach home or their intended locations directly. Unfortunately, they find themselves stuck on the bus. Consequently, some of them miss their appointments.

In a similar manner, many of us are dressed up and ready at God's terminal, anticipating the transport provided by God to take us to our respective destinations, referred to as destiny. Dressing up involves engaging in self-development activities that help our projection, such as attending school, learning a craft, or patiently praying and waiting for God's intervention in a hopeless situation. But sadly, some people lack patience, so they end up in unpleasant circumstances because they rush into anything to get going.

The best way to take advantage of the uncertainty of life is to prepare yourself. Opportunity will definitely come for everything a person wants to be; all they need to do is to prepare and wait for the opportunity. Anything done before the right time has the possibility of a major pitfall.

14

SELF-DETERMINATION

My philosophy is built on a mindset and determination that if there is only one man that would stand, I will be that one man. This does not mean that I am selfish, but the game is, if you are determined like I am, then we are a tie, and if everyone is determined like we are, then we are one indivisible team that would stand.

The ability to succeed is structured and strengthened by one's frame of mind and self-determination to stand against all odds for the right objective, not minding who gives up before him and around him. The success of a group is determined by the success of every individual in the group, and in the case of a failing group, one reserves the absolute right to achieve individual success within such a group.

In this society, immorality, insanity, and stupidity are celebrated, and a significant percentage of its inhabitants are drunks, dupes, or drug addicts. Moreover, many of our representatives in Government lack moral values and require relegation to a mental asylum. We are witnessing an era where abnormalities are being normalised, while reasonable ideologists are unfairly labelled as unreasonable. The acceptable standards and norms are becoming obsolete due to the lack of patronage. Remember, "That everybody does it does not mean it is right."

Some time ago, the late Nelson Mandela decided to stand against all odds for social equality and the restoration of human rights in South Africa. He stood, lived and died for it. The celebration of his life at his death by nations of the world is not just because he was a former president of South Africa, but because of his achievements which still ricochet wherever leadership ideology is discussed. Mandela stood up against a government that legalised an abominable act like apartheid. Though he was humiliated, ostracised, and imprisoned, yet he stood his ground. Everybody who shared his ideology, vision and passion joined him, and that great team still stands today.

No matter where you are, life is an unavoidable battle that we must face. As long as you still live, fight! Never give attention to those who have fallen because your survival in an enclosed city in war depends on your ability to fight till you win. Otherwise, you will die. Although you may be criticised, talked down, humiliated and discouraged, the ability to summon courage and move on is the only way to stand out, provided you are up for the right thing. No matter how eccentric it might look day by day, be the change you want to see.

15

GOOD THINGS HAVE A PRICE

A failure prays to God for honey and gets honeycombs, and then cries back to Him complaining that he had bees.

Every man who ever tasted or dined with success definitely had a rough side. I am talking of someone who lays the foundation of success that others around him are clinging on.

Honeycomb is the source of abundant honey. If God gives you a gallon of honey, He has only given you the resource from a honeycomb, which is limited and can finish anytime. When He gives you a honeycomb, you will definitely have to contend with the bees. But then, it is a source of unlimited flow of honey (the presence of the bees and the ability to manoeuvre them). A lot of people are in the category of individuals whom God has equipped with the tools and key to unveil a source of abundance, but some of them are busy bugging those who inherited resources and those who manage resources for others.

I was privileged to read an article about the founder of Cocominte, Nimrod, and was amazed by his story. At the age of four, he was already a contributor to his family upkeep. His first slippers, which he always wore to church, was an oversized gift from his uncle. According to him, education was not part of the family plan and budget. It was an adventure too far to imagine or undertake, considering their level of poverty. At that tender age, this only son amidst two daughters researched to understand the mystery of his existence through deeper and positive thinking on how to make a meaning out of life and, in turn, influence his family positively.

He would later realise that he was not a biological accident, but rather a perfectly programmed event by God which had to unfold. He realised that even though there was no honey in the house, God had given him a honeycomb. He began to manufacture the Cocominte drink right in his father's house. He would tie them in nylons, pour them in empty bottles, chilled them in a big cooler with ice blocks, and set out for business. He would strategically anchor under a mango tree where some construction workers were working, and before he mentioned "Jack-Robinson," the school children and construction workers had emptied his cooler. Sooner than later, the Chinese who were carrying out a construction project patronised his product. To his surprise, one of the Chinese, who was the project director, visited his home and solicited for a partnership in the Cocominte business. Today, Cocominte is a global brand, and Nimrod is the originator.

Just like Nimrod, a lot of us were not privileged to get gallons of honey but are fortunate to have honeycombs. Every good thing comes with a price.

16

THE RULE OF SUCCESS

In all human races, success obeys only one rule:
Do not give up.

If you want to succeed in life, you must never give up on yourself. You might face failure in a specific endeavour or direction, but there are other ways or entirely different paths where you can still succeed.

Several years ago, I had the privilege of working on a construction project owned by Exxon Mobil. During that time, there was a young boy of about my age who worked as a casual employee with Spibat and Fougerolle, the two civil construction companies in a joint venture for the project. He consistently approached me for a business partnership, but

I dismissed him, unable to mirror myself in the future he saw for himself at that age. All I cared about then was receiving my monthly salary, making some illicit money on the side, and going to the club to frolic with any good-looking prostitute who caught my eye.

However, two years later, this casual worker had already established his own company and actively participated in the construction of the Nigeria LNG project. Today, he owns a company where he employs expatriates. He never gave up; instead, he remained focused on achieving success.

By maintaining unwavering determination and fixing his eyes on success, he has become a shining example of how persistence and vision can lead to remarkable accomplishments.

17

TRIALS

Without trials, success will really be tasteless.

W e seldom take for granted anything that we suffer to attain. If you fail an examination five times, nobody will tell you to leap for joy the day you finally pass it, and nobody will tell you to treasure the result. The value attributed to success is dependent on the material, time, and psychological cost of achieving it.

A friend once shared a testimony about his elder sister with me while I was encouraging him to further his education. The testimony sounded funny but was very touching. I imagined myself in her shoes and felt the excitement in her spirit for success at last. She had sat for the Joint Admission and Matriculation Board (JAMB) Examination several times but could not hit the cut-off mark. JAMB is a prerequisite for gaining admission into Nigerian universities.

According to him, "On one of the occasions, about the second to the last attempt before she made it she just came back from where she went to check her result, without a single word to my mother or myself, she went straight to the fridge and picked a bottle of soft drink, and a half loaf of bread, sat with us in the sitting room and finished the half loaf of bread and the soft drink while we dumbfoundedly watched her. When she was done, she got up without words and went straight into her room.

"At this point, my mother had become a little bit troubled by her unusual behaviour, so she followed her to find out what was wrong. But on getting there, she had locked herself in and was crying uncontrollably. All effort to get her to open the door proved abortive. Since we could hear her cry, we didn't bother so much again knowing that at least, she was alive and crying. Much later in the evening, she came out and broke the news of her JAMB failure. We all pitied her. Days later, after she had recovered from the trauma, I asked her why all the pantomime and melodrama that preceded the divulgence of her poor result. She said she was trying to tell herself that she was probably dreaming and needed to wake up, so she tried to do some other things that mattered to her which was to put something in her empty stomach, believing that by the time she finished eating, maybe she would have woken from the dream, but unfortunately it was not a dream.

"It was then it dawned on her that she had failed again, and she could not afford to break the sad news to us there and then. The following year, she sat for the examination again. And on her return from where she went to check the result, she came with a pack of roasted plantain, opened the fridge, brought out a pack of juice, and helped herself again. After all that, she shouted enthusiastically and shared her success story."

The tough and demanding aspect of every success makes it more intriguing. When a success is achieved without encountering any challenges or difficulties, the feeling of accomplishment will not be as meaningful or fulfilling. Going through trials or difficult experiences is necessary for personal growth. It is also crucial to developing the skills and resilience needed to achieve success. Without these challenges, success may feel empty or unsatisfying because you have not earned it through hard work and perseverance. Therefore, the value we place on the things we need are based on the price we pay for them.

18

THE IMPOSSIBLE IS POSSIBLE

Success is more fascinating when achieved
through a long and rugged journey,
and in a vehicle tagged "impossible".

The victory of Donald Trump in the 2016 United States of America's presidential election was one that defied the world's expectation. I told a friend that Trump would probably isolate himself in his office after he announced the winner, asking himself, "How on earth did I get here against all odds?" Rejected by his own coalition, dumped by his allies, denigrated by foes, and blackmailed with his ignorant past, yet, he won. This kind of success is the type that marvels the achiever, a success that makes an achiever sit back in astonishment while reflecting on how they landed at it after all.

A great man of God once shared a story about a prophecy he gave to an old woman, which seemed ridiculous and impossible. The entire congregation he was ministering to didn't believe it because there was no visible evidence to suggest its materialisation. His host was so embarrassed that they had to discuss the matter after his ministration. They mentioned how the church was already taking care of her needs due to her poor condition and explained the reasons why it would be impossible for her to become a landlady in the United Kingdom as he had prophesied.

You know, God has mastery in embarrassing His servants with weird prophecies that would eventually become an overwhelming reality.

During the grand finale of the programme on the following Sunday, all the ministers were seated comfortably, hardly keeping in mind the rancorous outcomes of the previous days. Some members queued up for their testimonies, and as the progression continued the old woman joined the queue. Upon seeing her, the man of God felt like hiding himself. But the woman's testimony surprisingly revealed that she was now a landlady in the UK. The church turned upside down. This was a woman who could hardly afford a cup of garri. She had now become a house owner. What a pleasant twist of fate! Her children, who had abandoned her on the grounds that she was a witch as told by a supposed prophet, realised it was a false prophecy. So, one of her daughters tearfully gave her a house she had received as a gift from her husband there in the UK just to apologise for all they had done to her.

Success receives more accolades when it overrides all negative beliefs of men. And it is more fascinating when it is achieved on 1% possibility against 99% impossibility.

19

SUCCESS AND FAILURE

The amount of fascination attached to every success is weighed and evaluated by the activities that characterise the turning point where it overpowers failure.

W hen discussing success and failure in any given circumstance, they represent two distant and opposite ends that can never meet. The gaps between these two phenomena vary in each situation and within individual experiences.

One notable instance of unparalleled success took place in September 2013, when Diana Nyad, a 64-year-old American, achieved a historic feat. She became the first person to swim across the Florida Straits from Kuba without the protection of a shark cage. What made her achievement even more fascinating was her age and the fact that she had previously failed in four attempts.

Another remarkable example is Dr. Ben Carson, a retired neurosurgeon affiliated with John Hopkins Hospital. He had an outstanding academic record that serves as a benchmark for medical students at Yale University to this day. Dr. Carson was the first Neurosurgeon to successfully separate conjoined twins, and both of them survived. However, the most captivating aspect of his success lies in his teenage years, when he managed to transform from a failing position to a first-class position within a year.

Indeed, the ability to succeed during a significant mission, where every conventional means of success appears futile, makes the success story all the more interesting.

20

SPEND YOUR TIME WISELY

There is no crime in wishing that a day should be faster than normal, but the only ignorance is that as many times as you wished it and had it; you had drawn closer to your grave as much fast as that.

If you ask an average young man how long he intends to stay around, he will tell you that he wants to grow old. If you ask an average old man whose bones are still strong and his supplies are steady the same question, he will tell you that he wants to still be around for a while. Everybody wants to make the most of every day. When a day is pleasurable, everybody wishes that it does not pass by, but when it is not in our favour, we wish that it could be fast-forwarded.

A certain footballer striving to score a goal

got a long pass from his teammate. He went after the ball with eyes on it and finally got it, but unfortunately, he followed the ball across the touch line, and the referee blew his whistle over the bar. Sometimes, we run after our targets with our eyes fixed on them, desiring that hours could wind down to seconds so that we can quickly reach our goal. When we reach the goal, we realise that a lot of time has just passed. We realise that we have spent some reasonable time around. Years have passed us by, and we didn't seem to know. Though we got what we wanted, it was at the expense of our time on earth. We didn't know that while we were stomping our feet on the floor, wishing that time should fly in favour of the set date for our dream projects, we were invariably growing older as time flew, and by extension, we were drawing closer to our graves. Our lifelines and activities on earth are shortened by the second.

The emphasis here is on the preciousness and finiteness of time as regards our earthly timeline. Such a wish that a day should pass quickly is not inherently wrong, but it is a form of ignorance because every time we do so, we are essentially wishing for our lives to pass by more quickly and bring us closer to our deaths.

The quote is a warning against taking time for granted and to recognise the value of each, moment we have in life.

If you wish that your four years in the university should pass as quickly as five days can, take note that four years out of your life span would have been compressed into just four days if it were possible.

Psalm 90:12 (NIV) says, *"Teach us to number our days, that we may gain a heart of wisdom."* This verse serves as a reminder of the brevity of human life and the importance of using our time wisely. It encourages us to be mindful of the limited time we have on this earth and to seek wisdom in how we spend it.

21

CREDIT PURCHASES

The obsession for credit purchases has two probabilities: paying more for what you need or paying less for what you will never need.

This nugget highlights the repercussions of a culture or society that heavily emphasises credit purchases. The term "obsession for credit purchases" refers to the constant reliance on credit to make purchases, whether through direct credit buying, credit cards, loans, or other forms of borrowing.

The habit of buying things on credit may lead to self-deception, as individuals spend their future in the present, leaving nothing to rely on when that future eventually arrives. The mirage of such a lifestyle lies in the fact that people will consistently exhaust their future resources now unless they take the initiative to restrain themselves.

There are two potential outcomes of the obsession with credit purchases:

Paying more for what you need refers to the idea that when people buy on credit, they may end up paying more than the actual cost of the purchased item due to the item's profit margin, interest, or fees. This can happen when people buy an item to pay in future time, carry a balance on their credit cards or take out loans with high interest rates.

Paying less for what you will never need refers to the idea that people may use credit to buy things they don't actually need, or that they won't use in the future. In these cases, the person may get a good deal on the item when they buy it, but they will still be paying for something that they don't really need or use.

Credit is packaged in different ways in different places. In a well-developed society, it is packaged with a seeming sophistication to increase attraction and patronage. In these societies, credit eligibility is based on a steady source of income, and patrons can apply for credit cards through their banks, which enable them to make purchases to the limit of their financial worth determined by their incomes and what the bank is willing to offer. This gives them a licence to keep eating what they have not earned, driving cars their presents cannot afford, living in houses at the expense of their future, and living in luxuries that place huge demands on their futures.

In some societies, credits come in the form of loans obtainable from financial institutions like banks and loan houses. On the other hand, low earners in rural areas tend to visit shops where they make purchases on credit, with the intention to pay at a future date, often depleting their salaries before the end of the month. However, this apparent excess of resources conceals certain pitfalls related to credit eligibility and interest. Individuals may be tempted to buy things they believe they might need solely because they are cheap even though they might not actually use those items in the end.

Have you ever been to a shop to get some chicken pies where a waitress beams a smile at you and offers you some experimental snack for free if you can buy an extra chicken pie? That's more like it. A little more money for what you may never appreciate, and they pay because they are able. That is exactly what most people do when they have an extra coin. When such people run into any major financial challenge in the future that demands more than their depleted future income, they are usually subjected to paying a more demanding price to access what will enable them to deal with the situation.

If you want to know how hopeless a credit lifestyle could be, exhaust your credit value, go to the same bank that offered you credit facility and present a house or a car you bought with the facility to them as collateral for another credit to solve an urgent need that ordinarily is worth less than the value of the car or house. You will be shocked at the value they will make of whatever you present before them.

This nugget basically underscores the potential drawback of an obsession with credit purchases. While credit can serve as a valuable tool for managing finances and making purchases, it can also result in excessive debt and financial strain when not used responsibly. Living a credit-dependent life is akin to residing in a fool's paradise, as it entails a footing a lifestyle that may ultimately lead one into destitution.

22

DARE TO DREAM

The problem with most people is not the inability to pray, but rather a feeling of self-debasement that makes them shy away from the magnificent doors God opens before them in answer to their supplications.

A man could be as great as every great vision that comes into his mind but by choice. Today, you cannot talk about the origin of aeroplanes without mentioning the Wright Brothers. But several years ago, it was just an imagination in their minds which they could have seen as impossible. After all, some people still think it is a white man's witchcraft, otherwise how could it fly without flapping its wings?

I only imagined the phobia and fatality associated with learning how to drive when I thought of the need to create a facility where people could drive in a room until they were good enough to drive on roads. Then God gave me an opening, and I might be the first person to open a simulator driving school in Port Harcourt because I imagined it and believed it was possible.

The truth is that genuine imaginations can become realities. If you can imagine the creation of the earth on the surface of water and the suspension of heaven without pillars, then you can imagine how powerful our God is. Now, imagine that you are made like Him with the ability for self-development and environmental development for your comfort and fulfilment in His creation.

Do you know that in His master plan to make you an earthly being to till the ground, Genesis chapter 2 verses 5 to 7 speaks of the ability for development and the ability to work on His provided resources for the enrichment of the earth? Do you know that every great imagination that comes to your mind is in line with 'tilling' the earth? And when you make no effort to do so, you are denying the essence of your being.

Matthew 13:12 says, *"Whoever has will be given more, and he will have abundance. Whoever does not have, even what he has will be taken from him."*

Every picture God puts in your mind can become a reality via your interest and commitment to birth it. It can make you swim in abundance, and it can also leave you when you are afraid to work on it. You could be as great as the great pictures God pictures in your mind.

Most times our limitation is a product of fear and lack of self-confidence, and not because what is before us or in our mind is not realistic. Someone once said, "Your greatness begins in your dream; your impoverishment starts the moment you let it die."

23

WEALTH IS A BY-PRODUCT OF SOLUTIONS

Don't search for wealth if you truly desire one because you may lose track. Instead, search for challenges to solve; they are the nuts that birth true wealth.

Wealth is accessed by an exchange power that presents itself as challenges. Every challenge of a society is an open cheque to wealth but you can only write on it the worth of the solution you proffer to such a challenge. No matter how long you hunger and search for wealth, you can never find it until you create an exchange factor. Those who command wealth today created an avenue for it through the provision of a service or product. An unrestrained desire for wealth coupled with laziness in creating services or products as a means of wealth exchange will invariably result in financial crime.

Money does not stroll on the street or grow on trees; it is in the custody of individuals and the government. The only way to obtain it from them is to give them something they need. Today, the world is facing an economic recession; however, those with essential products and services are cashing out. This sage emphasises the idea that one should not chase money or other material possessions per se. Instead, the focus should be on overcoming challenges and solving problems, as this is the true pathway to wealth.

If you can provide a solution to what your community needs, you are on the track to accessing wealth. There is a solution you can offer, even in times of scarcity, that would make a man who doesn't have to borrow in order to access the consuming right of what you have to offer.

Wealth is intended to be a byproduct of addressing the difficult challenges that afflict our society. This implies that genuine wealth is not solely confined to money or material possessions but is rather determined by the life challenges one successfully resolves. In essence, if an individual concentrates solely on the pursuit of wealth, they may become excessively preoccupied with this endeavour and consequently lose sight of what is genuinely significant in life.

Seek out challenges to solve, as they provide opportunities for personal growth, learning and development. And these experiences give rise to a sense of fulfilment and satisfaction, which can be considered as a form of true wealth. Nuts are difficult to crack, but they contain valuable and nourishing elements on the inside. Similarly, while challenges can be tough to overcome, they offer valuable opportunities for growth and development, and by extension, wealth creation. Focus on the journey of solving challenges and view wealth as a byproduct of that journey, rather than as the ultimate goal.

24

A CONSCIENTIOUS PERSON

A conscientious man weighs a gift not with the scale of his hunger, but with the scale of emotion of the giver and the opportunity cost on him.

Conscientious or considerate people do not evaluate gifts based on their personal desires or needs, but based on the emotions of the giver and the potential cost to the giver.

Some time ago, one of my acquaintances invited me to his wedding, and when I checked the date, I knew there was no way I could make it due to my schedule. I told him that but promised to send him my gift. He called a few days after the wedding, and I asked him to send me his bank account number which he did almost at once. Knowing the financial need around him as a young man who just got married, I could not wait until a future date to send something to him. I had to transfer a token into his account, which was all that I had at that moment.

When he called me later and I told him what I had done, he reacted in a seemingly ungrateful manner. He lamented, "Oooh! Sir, that account is in debit. Whatever you have done would first of all settle the minimum required balance and may not remain enough for me after all to deal with what I have at hand."

I felt so bad that I felt his pain, but he did not feel mine. He also didn't have to impoverish the sacrifice I made because of the size of his challenge. If a man forfeits his one meal for you and starves all day because that's all he had to eat for the day, his meal should be placed, on the scale of sacrifice above a thousand dollars gift from a millionaire.

The phrase "scale of hunger" refers to the recipient's level of desire for the gift and the size of the challenge they anticipate resolving with the money, while the "scale of emotion of the giver" denotes the amount of thought, time, and effort the giver invested in the gift. The "opportunity cost" refers to the cost to the giver in terms of the alternatives they could have chosen to spend their time, money, or resources on instead.

A conscientious person will take into account not only the size of their wants or needs and the amount they are gifted in relation to their needs, but also the feelings of the giver and the cost to the giver. This shows empathy and gratitude to the giver's actions, and ensures that the gift is valued and appreciated in the way that the giver intended.

25

INTEGRITY

*Integrity is my real weight and worth; my
reputation depends on your scale.*

Various factors contribute to why certain
people may not perceive you as your true self.
And their perspective plays a significant role
in shaping their opinion about how they see
you.

You are often susceptible to misjudgement
when situations play out openly among those
who may not benefit from your firm stance or
when upholding integrity demands that you
stand against the majority.

If you are confident that your internal values
align with a strong moral stance, your
judgements and positions are rational, and

your perspective remains unaffected by transferred aggression or past impressions, then it is essential to move on. In life, we all perceive things through different lenses. Some view the world through moral lenses, while others see it through corrupted lenses.

A lot of things are factored into peoples' perspective about you. Some may be right about you while some don't just have a sense of good things. While some are misinformed about you, others are just envious and jealous.

My true value and importance are rooted in my integrity and moral character. Although I believe that my reputation is closely tied to my integrity, there is a risk of being misunderstood and misjudged. In other words, if you have a negative perception of someone, it might be inaccurate. I invite you to approach them with an open mind, free from bias, to genuinely understand their disposition and intentions.

26

LOVE

Love will always find a way to be heard; even in the worst scenarios, she speaks without words.

Love possesses a remarkable quality; sometimes, it appears even more beautiful under pretence. I wonder if others have sensed this too. It is more vocal without words. Give it a try. Have you ever pondered how the deaf and dumb express love? They convey it with greater intensity than spoken words, and they hear it more clearly than sound.

Love is the only illuminating force that can effortlessly transcend any cover to reach an intending heart. It communicates in many languages, and one of them is smiles. Astonishingly, regardless of your origin or where it comes from, love addresses you in a language you can understand.

Love remains a powerful force that cannot be silenced, even in challenging circumstances. When verbal communication falters and is impossible, love will find ways to express itself through actions, gestures, and other nonverbal means. Even in the worst situations, love will still make itself known and felt. It is a universal language that surpasses words and has the ability to bridge any barrier, making sure its voice is heard, felt, and understood.

27

ANGER

The harvest of anger destroys the seed of peace.

This nugget is a metaphorical statement that suggests that when people act out of anger, they can cause harm to the prospects of achieving peace.

As written in Proverbs 15:18, a hot-tempered person stirs up conflict, but the one who is patient calms a quarrel. Similarly, Proverbs 29:11 states that "fools give full vent to their rage, but the wise bring calm in the end."

When people are consumed by anger, it has destructive outcomes. Anger can be likened to a harvest that controls a person's thoughts and actions, prompting them to act in non-peaceful and unconstructive ways. In contrast, the seed of peace represents the potential of a peaceful resolution. However, when anger is allowed to grow unchecked, it destroys this potential for reconciliation.

Secondly, imagine a farmer who has sown seeds of peace, aiming to nurture a crop of understanding and harmony. If that farmer permits anger to thrive within him and yields to it, he may ultimately destroy the very crop he had aspired to harvest. The destructive force of anger can unravel all the commendable work that had been undertaken towards cultivating peace.

One challenging aspect of moments of anger is the belief that expressing it towards your contender would provide relief. Ironically, 99.9% of the words spoken in anger only act as a catalyst to a shocking reaction from the recipient of your anger. And this cycle may continue until both parties have said and done things that are deeply hurtful and hard to let go. Even if forgiveness is eventually granted, the knowledge that such low thoughts and actions were expressed can cause a permanent rift, leading them to distance themselves from you forever. Therefore, controlling one's words and actions during moments of anger is crucial.

Unguided statements and reactions can lead to the exposure of secrets, the accumulation of pressure, the growth of hatred, and viewing each other as monsters. You can, however, avoid these consequences by managing your anger, as history shows that great people have fallen because of anger. Marriages have also broken due to irrevocable words uttered in fits of anger. Don't become a victim of anger.

In a broader context, succumbing to anger can lead individuals to inflict harm and destruction on the peaceful relationships they have worked hard to build with others. This serves as a cautionary message, reminding us not to let our emotions rule our actions. It also reminds us of the significance of cultivating a mindset centred on peace and understanding.

28

RISING LATE

The challenge I have with rising late is that you may never have all the time you need, or you may never have all the rest you need.

Rising late symbolises the realisation of one's potential and purpose at a later stage in life, and coming to terms with what should have been accomplished much earlier but was carelessly neglected.

Many people waste their youthful and fruitful years on frivolous pursuits, only to awaken to the reality of their abilities and talents much later in life. Growing up in a community where the highest potential for young individuals was limited to apprenticeships or learning crafts for survival,

I was distracted from recognising my true calling. If I had known the significance of education in my vocation, I would have prioritised it above everything else I did to make a living; I would have covered much more miles than I am currently.

Similarly, if I had understood the inevitability of salvation through Jesus Christ and the abundance of privileges and potentials that come with a relationship with Him, I would have embraced Christianity long ago. I would have already overcome some of the challenges that young Christians often face, and I would have grown more deeply in my faith.

Learn from this lesson: do things at the right time to prevent reaching a point where you feel overwhelmed or in a hurry to achieve them.

29

SEED OF GREATNESS

Every seed of greatness is handcuffed by criticism,
jailed by ridicule, and isolated by the hideous looks
of failure. If you must realise your full potential,
you must disarm these foes.

There are three major forces you must deal with at the start of every undertaken with great potential:

Number one is criticism. You would be told how wrongly you have started by people who feel they know better even when they know nothing. I quite agree that some criticisms are objective, but some are mere rigmaroles to get you confused and frustrated.

Number two is ridicule. People are so used to little things and little visions so much that when your vision is great, no matter your measure to accomplishing it, until it becomes reality, it is not everybody that would believe it realisation.

I have a friend who now owns a company employing expatriates. I distinctly recall the day he walked into my office back in 2002 on a sunny afternoon. He was sweating profusely from the intense heat of the sun and looked noticeably emaciated. He had with him a ten-million-naira document, seeking my involvement in his business. To be honest, everything about his proposal and claim seemed implausible, considering his appearance and the apparent emptiness that hovered around him.

The people we look up to with our great proposals often underestimate our ability to drive them, especially when there is no structural background to support our intentions. This underestimation can be humiliating and may even lead one to give up on a quest that should have succeeded.

The third force that hunts the start-up of a great venture is the fear of failure. The fear of uncertainty has swallowed a lot of potentials. Many have given up on projects that could have transformed their societies due to the fear of failure that engulfs them each time they look at the distance between their startups and the realisation of their dreams. As a result, they allow the spirit of self-debasement to stop them from daring it.

The potential for greatness in each person is often hindered by negative factors. These factors can act like handcuffs, limiting a person's potential and preventing them from achieving their goals. To unlock one's potential for greatness, one must disarm these obstacles by overcoming the fear of criticism, ridicule, and failure. By doing so, one can free themselves from these constraints and allow their full potential to grow and flourish. The quote emphasises the importance of perseverance, resilience, and self-belief in achieving goals, even in the face of adversity.

If you want to succeed in life, you must disregard criticisms that are designed to slow you down. Don't mind those who say you can't do it; believe in yourself and your dream. Lastly, keep your eyes off failure and focus on the objective.

30

WILLPOWER

The greatest power against your success is not the power of darkness, but the power of will.

The ability to do anything lies in the conception of its possibility. The first place to conquer any war is in the mind, not in might. As a matter of fact, might most times could be a reflection of inner strength, courage, and willpower. The best thing God created in your earthly body is your mind. An active mind propels faith, and faith is the life wire that ignites your will to do anything you need to do and to be whatever you need to be. Stop grumbling about the resources that are not within your reach and focus on the sources within you. You can never be successful without your approval. Men can move your hands to do something for you, but no one can move your mind to mine the treasury within you. That's the truth.

The biggest impediment to success does not stem from external factors like challenges, opposition, or obstacles. Instead, it lies in the potency of your own will or motivation. Strong willpower and motivation are imperative in surmounting obstacles and achieving your goals. While external factors may pose a risk, it is up to you to choose how you respond to those challenges. And when you have a strong will, you can easily overcome them.

Your mindset and determination play pivotal roles in achieving success, and the absence of strong willpower can pose a significant obstacle to reaching your goals. In the end, the influence of your own will surpass that of any external factors when it comes to determining your success.

31

MARRIAGE

*The hard side of marriage is that people make it
hard on themselves.*

This quote implies that the challenges or difficulties encountered in a marriage often arise from the actions or choices made by the individuals involved in the relationship. In other words, it is not necessarily the institution of marriage itself that is inherently difficult, but rather the behaviours and attitudes of the spouses that can lead to tensions and problems.

In obvious ways, we all contribute to the problems that arise in our respective marriages through our actions, behaviours, or attitudes. We possess control over how we handle our relationships, and our choices can either facilitate or complicate matters. Thus, the difficult side of marriage is not an inherent characteristic of marriage itself, but rather a result of how people approach and navigate their relationship.

Every marriage demands effort, compromise, and the willingness to take responsibility for one's actions. Each part has a role to play in making the relationship a successful union.

32

FRIENDSHIP

*Our prospects are far richer than our presents,
and a heart of friendship will make the custodian
one of us.*

The main problems with Joseph's brothers were selfishness, ignorance of the fact that they couldn't hinder his destiny, and failure to see the need for his friendship in the future. Ironically, many of us today still fall into this trap of "me versus everyone else" mentality. Embracing a more liberal approach in our quests in life rather than being self-centred is a safer and wiser choice.

While striving for success and individual recognition is essential, it is crucial not to adopt a competitive attitude that may strain opportunities to form lasting friendships.

Some of us tend to be myopic, believing the world revolves around us and deeming others worthless until they achieve success. We often forget that life is a progressive journey.

Our relationships are like seeds that we sow, and they will eventually bear fruit (either good or bad). Therefore, it is critical to sow seeds of kindness and consideration that we will be proud to harvest in the future. Cultivating opportunities for friendship and kindness can make success our close neighbour, as every act of kindness is a seed that will eventually bear fruit.

The most effective approach to invest in an unpredictable tomorrow is through kindness towards others, as their actions and reactions cannot be foreseen. Refrain from causing harm or hurting people simply because you have the capability to do so; instead, choose to be compassionate and considerate. Approach every individual with the mindset of a farmer sowing seeds into the ground: despite the difficulty of tilling the soil, the farmer releases his precious seeds, patiently awaiting the eventual harvest, regardless of how long it takes.

The future undoubtedly holds greater potential for abundance and success than the present, and nurturing strong relationships through friendship can pave the way to realising that potential. This approach suggests that those entrusted with safeguarding or managing our resources can contribute to our success when we treat them as allies and friends instead of adversaries. In summary, the focal point here is on the power of optimism, friendship, and collaboration to unlock greater opportunities for growth and prosperity.

33

THE MIND

Our minds are so powerful that at every point in time they get ahead of us to reach higher grounds that only courage, commitment, boldness and faith could take us to.

This nugget underscores the remarkable power and potential of our minds, highlighting the capacity of the human mind to envision and pursue greater heights in life. It also implies that our minds may outpace our current reality, continuously yearning for progress and advancement.

To bridge the gap between our present state and the higher grounds our minds conceive, the nugget highlights four vital qualities: courage, commitment, boldness, and faith. Let's explore the meaning of each of these qualities:

Courage: This refers to the ability to face and overcome fears, doubts, and obstacles that might arise on the path to reaching higher grounds. It involves the strength to step out of our comfort zones and take risks in order to pursue our aspirations.

Commitment: This quality underscores the importance of dedication and persistence. It implies that we must stay focused on our goals and be willing to put in consistent effort and hard work to turn our aspirations into reality.

Boldness: Being bold involves having the audacity to think and act in unconventional ways. It implies a willingness to challenge the status quo and take unconventional approaches to achieve our ambitions. Boldness encourages us to think outside the box and embrace innovation.

Faith: In this context, faith refers to the belief in ourselves and in the possibilities that lie ahead. It suggests maintaining a positive mindset, even in the face of setbacks or uncertainty. Having faith in our abilities and the potential for success can help propel us forward towards our goals.

Together, these qualities are essential attributes that can help us bridge the gap between our current reality and the higher grounds our minds aspire to reach. By embodying courage, commitment, boldness, and faith, we can harness the power of our minds to achieve extraordinary things and bring our visions to life.

34

HUNGER DRIVES DREAMS

Our capacity to dream is not subject to age or background, but interest and hunger, and our capacity to achieve our dreams is subject to the obedience to the principle of success.

Dreams are predominantly shaped by one's interests and desires, rather than one's age or background. Put simply, every mind has the capacity to conceive ideas related to areas in life that evoke one's interest or passion. While the magnitude of our dream may be influenced by our age and experiences, the crucial point remains: the ability to dream and aspire is not limited by age or background. Instead, it hinges on the depth of our interest and hunger for success.

This implies that anyone, irrespective of

their background or circumstances, can have daring dreams and goals if they possess enough passion and commitment.

However, the realisation of these dreams depends on our willingness to adhere to the principles of success. This implies that we must possess a clear understanding of what success means to us and the principles we must embrace to attain it. Some of these principles may encompass hard work, determination, perseverance, patience, focus, and learning from failures.

In essence, our dreams are attainable as long as we have the interest and hunger to pursue them. We must also be prepared to abide by the principles of success. It is up to us to take responsibility for our own success, and diligently work towards turning our dreams into reality, irrespective of our age or background.

35

DON'T COMPROMISE

It takes a fool to accept a peaceful resolution to the detriment of his godliness, and to adhere to a fusion at the expense of his morality, fundamental human right and self-actualisation.

It is unwise to accept a peaceful resolution that compromises one's own beliefs, values, and sense of self-actualisation. In the pursuit of peace or unity, some may be tempted to sacrifice their principles or moral code, which is not acceptable.

The phrase "his godliness" refers to a person's spiritual or religious beliefs and principles. Even in the pursuit of peace, one should not compromise their religious or spiritual beliefs, as it would come at the expense of personal integrity and morality.

Similarly, the phrase "fundamental human right" suggests that compromising on one's principles or values could also infringe on the rights and freedoms of others, which is not acceptable.

Any truce that demands compromising these four elements that define every human's self-actualisation calls for self-betrayal, enslavement, and, at worst, the soul. Daily confrontations may demand compromise and ungodly affiliation, leading to spiritual and physical attacks that disfranchise us from our fundamental human rights.

Sometimes, we are humiliated over our privileges in order to disorient our focus. Regardless of these, you must neither give in nor give up. Many people from different sectors of the society are entangled in all manners of compromising undertakings that ultimately bring nothing but regret and reproach to them.

In essence, it is important to maintain one's sense of morality even in the pursuit of peace or unity. Compromising one's beliefs and values would be a mistake. True peace and unity can only be achieved through mutual respect and understanding without sacrificing one's integrity.

36

BE THE BEST

*The best advertisement for what you do is
to be the best at it.*

It is natural for anyone to take pride in their actions and choices, but in the face of competition, true quality will eventually prevail. Often, during my commutes to and from work, I would stop at a particular place to enjoy some delicious bean cakes (akara) for breakfast or to bring some home for my wife. One day, I decided to patronise another woman, whom I had known for a while, and it turned out to be even better and tastier, as confirmed by my wife. Consequently, she effortlessly gained our loyalty to her product.

Some time ago, I needed to download a specific mobile application, and when I entered the phone's app store, I was faced with numerous options, making it challenging to choose. I resorted to reading the comments and experiences of other users who had previously used the app, hoping to make an informed decision through their referrals.

People tend to patronise things more based on word-of-mouth referrals than traditional advertising. The most effective way to promote what you do is to be really good at it. In other words, the quality of your work or product will speak for itself and naturally attract others to you.

There is no substitute for being excellent at what you do. Instead of relying solely on advertising or marketing, the best way to attract new customers, clients, or fans is to be known for your expertise and skills.

Strive for excellence in your work, and let that excellence be your advertisement. People are naturally drawn to quality work, and by focusing on your craft and continuously improving your skills, you will build a reputation that attracts new opportunities and clients. It is essential to recognise that word of mouth and personal recommendations are far more effective than traditional advertising in building a loyal following.

A good advertisement may be undermined by a bad product or service, but a good product or service without official advertising can sell unimaginably well based on referrals.

37

MEANINGFUL RELATIONSHIPS

The fact that I have never referenced your weakness does not mean you don't have them; they are mostly natural. And the fact that you always rub my nose over mine, is your choice; and that exactly is one of yours.

In a certain measure, every human being on earth has some elements of weakness; they could be attitudinal, mental, or emotional weaknesses informed by the environment, biological influences, family backgrounds, and orientations, as the case may be. Some very intelligent and kind-hearted people snore uncontrollably when they sleep; some are social, while others are introverts. Some people can't stop correcting others when they do wrong, while others don't care as long as it's not their business. Some are very selective when it comes to food, while others would eat anything as long as someone could survive on it. Some of these could be considered weaknesses, and on the other hand, they could also be strengths.

If we all come to terms with the reality that at every point in time, every one of us is being tolerated by the next person, it would become easier for us to manage our relationships with the people we meet in the course of life, and even in our marriages. Because when you think that there is something wrong with someone and, as a result, disparage them without considering the factors that may have contributed to their weaknesses, and without understanding how much effort they put up to overcome them, it suggests that you have a weakness of understanding. This is why you fail to empathise with people who make sincere efforts to overcome their weaknesses but need your understanding to strengthen them.

It is important for us to recognise our own weaknesses and take responsibility for our actions, rather than constantly pointing out the flaws of others. Understanding that our actions and choices reflect who we are as individuals is crucial for personal growth, and they reflect who we are as individuals.

38

CHALLENGES

*A challenge is just an introductory page of every
great and outstanding success story.*

One of the crucial elements of an interesting movie is the unfolding of suspenseful moments, known as the twist or climax. The story of every great individual that has ever existed had its own plotline, twists, and climaxes that set the stage for excitement.

A challenge before someone with the potential for greatness is like a thick, cloudy day that preludes the appearance of a rainbow. The difference between other birds and an eagle is that while the other birds hide their faces in their nests during adverse stormy weather, the eagle rides on the wind for a famous remark. Challenges are always problematic for everyone without an apparent solution.

When Nebuchadnezzar had a significant dream, forgot what he dreamt, and summoned his astrologers and magicians to remind him of the dream and interpret it for him, under the threat of a death penalty if they failed, it was an unprecedented and seemingly impossible task for all of them. Imagine how terrified these men must have been facing such an impossible task and the dehumanising conditions they were subjected to. But when Daniel heard of it, it was rather a moment of ovation for him (Daniel Chapter 2).

Challenges and obstacles are not only normal but also necessary for success. They are like the first page of a book; they mark the starting point of a great story. Just as every book has an introduction that sets the stage for the rest of the story, every success story has challenges that pave the way for the achievement of great things.

Do not give up in the face of challenges; you should rather see them as opportunities to grow and learn. Challenges can be daunting, but they can also be viewed as opportunities for growth, learning, and progress.

Success stories are not handed to people on a silver platter; they require hard work, perseverance, and determination. The challenges that arise along the way are simply part of the process of achieving something great. So, as you desire greatness, make up your mind to confront challenging situations and overcome them. Remember, there is always an element of greatness on the other side of every challenge.

39

GREATNESS IS NOT ACCIDENTAL

There will always be a traffic jam at the junction to the long street to glory, but every determined fellow would step out, and walk the lonely street to glory, just for a lone experience with glory.

Have you ever noticed that not everyone you grew up with measures up to where you are now, and vice versa? We often plan and strategise for our future. Greatness rarely happens by accident; it is usually fuelled by determination, propelled by vision, followed by preparation, and ultimately, driven by the right opportunities.

The path to greatness is not an easy one; it requires a level of distinctiveness to move ahead of others. Life and destiny are individualistic; don't get stuck comparing yourself to others, and don't settle for merely going through the motions. Strive to break through where others are stuck; that's the only way you can truly stand out. Those who push through where others give up are the ones destined for greatness, and those who achieve glory with a lone hand are those who go the extra mile. Set your sights on glory and leave no room for alternatives.

Metaphorically, the quest for achieving great things in life can be likened to travelling along the long street to glory, which is not an easy journey. The traffic congestion along the way represents the obstacles and challenges we encounter while pursuing our goals.

Although there will always be obstacles and challenges, those who remain resolute in their pursuits will find a way to overcome them. They will be willing to traverse the lonely street to glory, even if it means crawling, walking, and running alone, because the ultimate goal of attaining glory is worth the effort.

In essence, be persistent, dedicated, and willing to face challenges in order to achieve your goals. Success does not come easy, but it can be attained with determination and perseverance.

40

CAPACITY FOR GREATNESS

When it comes to greatness, God gives measures to every man according to his container.

Each one of us possesses a unique capacity for greatness, and the extent of our achievements in life is determined by the size of our individual container. In this context, container refers to our potential, capabilities, or willpower.

The ability to dream is a gift inherent in every individual. God has bestowed upon each of us creative ability in accordance with our being made in His image and likeness.

However, the breadth of our dreams is relative to our individual interests, and the extent to which we can pursue those dreams is influenced by our willpower and God's intervention through His law of sowing and reaping. The foundation of greatness is first laid in the mind; the bricks that construct the realisation of greatness are moulded in our thoughts and carefully assembled day by day until we reach the pinnacle of achievement. We all have the licence and mental capacity to exceed our structural limitations.

Every remarkable accomplishment you witness today once existed only in the mind of someone who may not have had all the privileges you enjoy today. These achievements may have been accomplished by individuals who were least regarded by society and never expected to dream of anything significant. Resist conforming to mediocrity, as it corrodes the innovative fibres of those around you. Instead, develop your mental strength to break free from the confines of limitations.

The ability to reach our desired heights in life is fuelled by our individual willpower, coupled with God's favour. In essence, each of us is unique and possesses our own distinct capacity for greatness. We should strive to reach our full potential without comparing ourselves to others, as our potential for greatness is individual and incomparable to anyone else's.

I trust *The Epiphanies* has blessed you.

You can contact the author through any of the details below:

Email:

graciousfount@gmail.com

Facebook:

Gracious Fount

Mobile:

+23480 388 69991 or +234 90 144 20005